To my dear Jai and Kish— who inspired this book and drive me to bring more culture to our lives.

To Samit— who supports my visions and dreams.

To Mom, Dad, Mummy, and Papa— who enable our culture in our home and hearts.

And to my loving sibs and sibs-in-law— who support me and show me unconditional love.

Hi, my name is Jaiyen. I am 5 and I live in Chicago.

It's nice to meet you!

My little brother Kishyn is 3. Together we are starting our Diwali celebrations at home. My family is Indian and American, and Diwali is a really special time for us.

We want to share it with you.

Will you celebrate Diwali with us?

Shine a Light on Diwali

on Diwali

Written by Parul L. Bhandari

ISBN: 978-1-958150-49-8
Shine a Light on Diwali:
An American-born, Indian-Heritage Family
Celebrates the Festival of Lights

First publication: October 2024

Published by **Inner Peace Press**
Eau Claire, Wisconsin, USA
www.innerpeacepress.com

Diwali is usually in the fall. I remember it's around Halloween. It is also called the Festival of Lights. Diwali is a time when people celebrate good over bad, light over dark. My Mama says it's like when the good guys beat the bad guys in my favorite superhero stories, and everyone celebrates.

In this case, the good guys are a few brothers named Rama and Laxmana, and their friend Hanuman, the Monkey King. They defeated a bad guy named Ravana, and rescued the princess Sita from him. I love that Rama and Laxmana are brothers like me and Kishyn.

During diwali we do a lot! We meet with family, do a puja, visit friends, eat lots of yummy food, and, my favorite part, we light sparklers!!

We started the Diwali weekend by cleaning our house, and decorating with our parents. Diwali is a time for new beginnings in a way, so we always clean our homes and prepare them for good energy. After cleaning, we start decorating as well. While my Mama and Papa were trying to untangle a bunch of string lights, Kishyn and I put plastic orange flowers on our staircase.

Mama and Papa say that the lights and decorations will allow the good energy of the Diwali season to find us in our home, so the more the better. We also put diyas with small candles in them all over the house.

Diyas are small lamps, usually made with clay and filled with hot oil. This year we made diyas out of colorful molding dough, and decorated them with sparkly gem stickers. Our diyas do not burn your hands like some candles do because they use batteries. My brother Kishyn put sooo many gem stickers all over his diyas, but mine just had a few.

Later that afternoon, Nana and Nani, our grandparents, came over to make Diwali treats, called laddoos. We like to take laddoos to school and to share them with our neighbors. During Diwali, we usually visit friends and share sweets, my second favorite part!

Nani was stirring a big pot of flour made of chickpeas mixed with sugar and ghee, which made the house smell like a nutty cookie. When she was done, she put a big bowl of sweet and warm laddoo mix on the table on a paper towel.

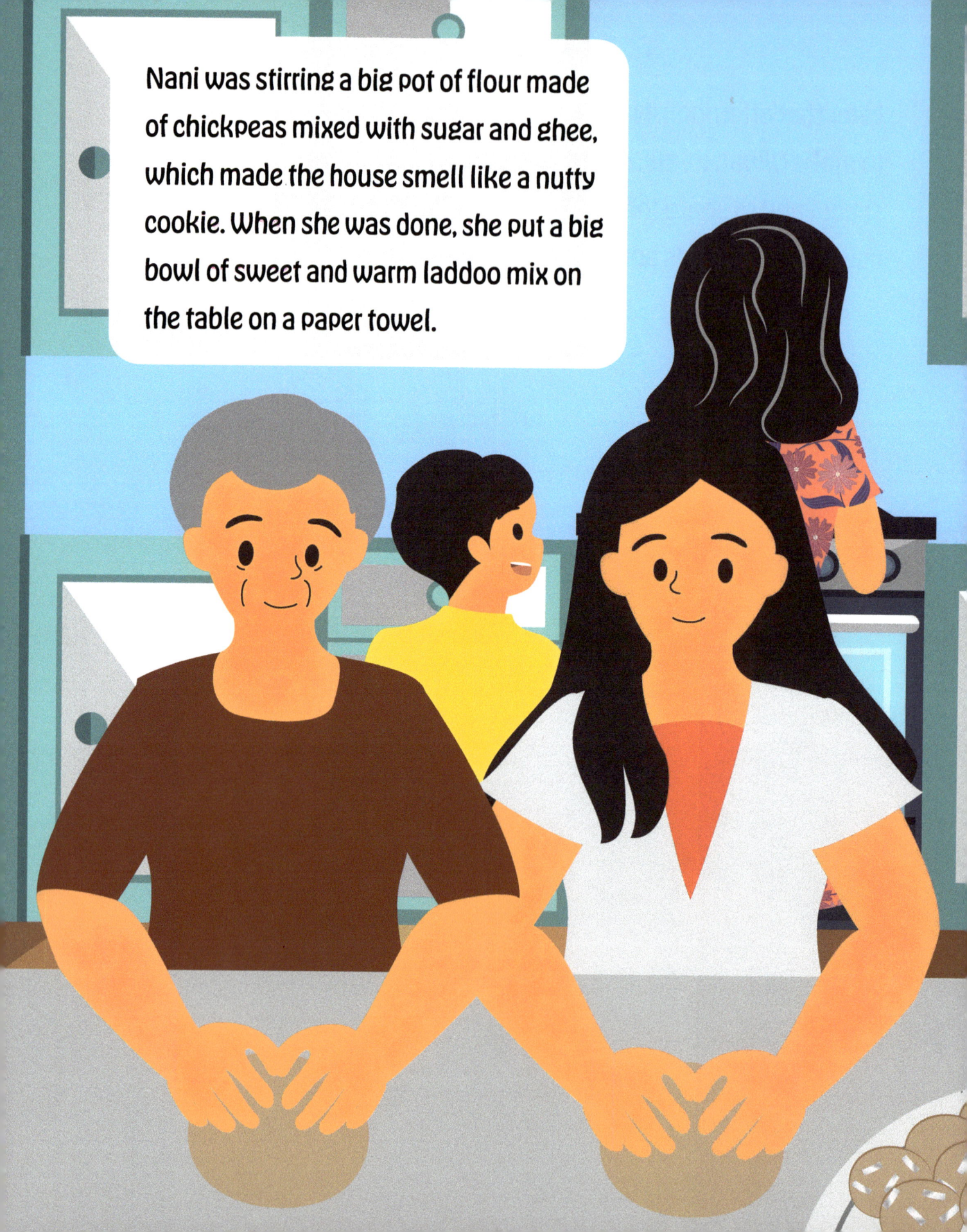

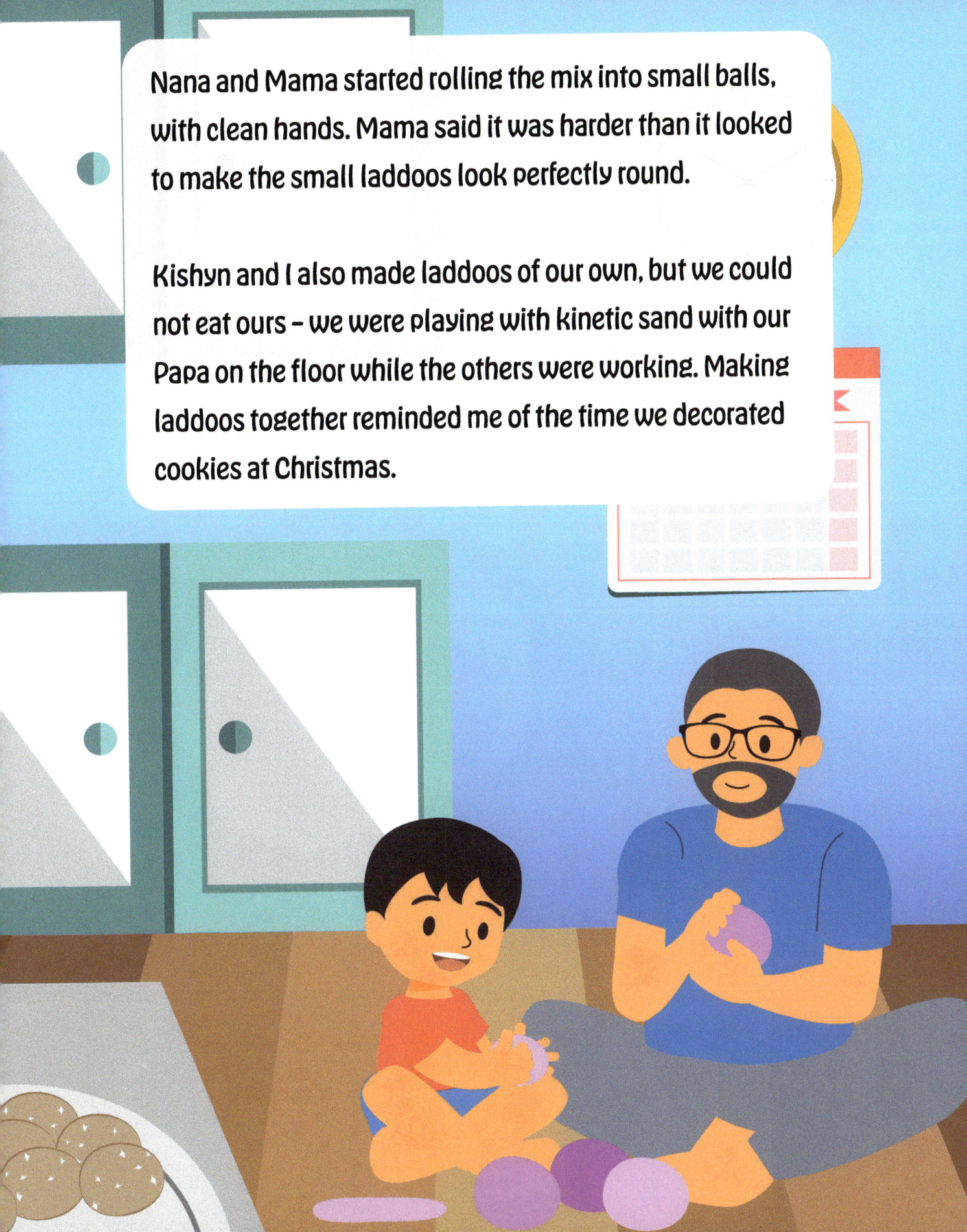

Nana and Mama started rolling the mix into small balls, with clean hands. Mama said it was harder than it looked to make the small laddoos look perfectly round.

Kishyn and I also made laddoos of our own, but we could not eat ours – we were playing with kinetic sand with our Papa on the floor while the others were working. Making laddoos together reminded me of the time we decorated cookies at Christmas.

When Mama and Papa finished, Kishyn and I washed hands and got to top all the laddoos with tiny sprinkles or silver foil – Kishyn ate so many sprinkles during the process... I did too. Mama packed up some laddoos and gold chocolate coins (my third favorite) into small boxes for gifts. I asked who we were packing them for and Mama said it was a gift for our neighbors. Soon, it was getting to be dinner time so we finished decorating and ate a quick dinner of roti roll-ups, wraps made of roti and sabji. It was a super busy day, and we all went to sleep soon after.

The next day, we had a Diwali party with our neighbors, Jordan, Taylor, Sachin, and Reyna, and my cousins Parisa and Pasha. They are all my best friends and live right in the neighborhood. We ate pizza, samosas, had laddoo treats, played games, and did some Diwali coloring. After a while, we all went out to do some sparklers. This is something special we do with our neighbors every year and it's so fun. After sparklers we all had to go to bed for the start of a busy week of school.

A few days later, my Mama, Papa, Kishyn, and I wore special Indian clothes... to school! This was not a normal day, we were celebrating Diwali with my class. I usually only dress up at school on picture day or on a presentation day, like holiday assembly.

I got dropped off and a little later my family came into class with some other parents. We read a Diwali book, talked about how we celebrate Diwali at home, and we even decorated diyas with my class.

We shared laddoos with the class and another Mama poured mango lassi, a sweet mango yogurt smoothie. Some of the kids in my class said they had the most fun doing the diya project, and that made me feel so happy.

After a while, Mama, Papa, and Kishyn had to leave. I was glad they came and that we had a lot more Diwali fun to come.

Friday was the real "Diwali Day" according to my parents, so guess what – I stayed home from school, and so did Kishyn. Mama and Papa were home all day, and spent the morning setting up for our puja. Puja is a time we ask for blessings for Diwali for our home, our family, and for the year ahead. We had a lot of people over that day – our cousins, aunts and uncles, and grandparents.

During the puja, Dada, my other grandpa, lets Kishyn and I wash the Ganesha and Laxmi statues, and cover them with milk and honey. Mama says we are taking God to get a facial, which everyone laughs at. Nana laughs and says, but really during the puja we are doing cleansing rituals for our statues to prepare them for the prayer we will do, and the cleansing is called Abhishekam (uh - bhee-sh-ehk-um). We also do Abhishekam on some coins which Dada has had in his family for over 100 years. Dadi, my other grandma, says these coins are very special because they are being passed down over generations.

Then we sing bhajans, or prayer songs, as a family, led by my Bua – she is my dad's sister and has a pretty voice. I don't always understand all the words, but I love singing songs together. Kishyn sings very loud sometimes, it's funny. Masi and Masa, my aunt and uncle, and my cousins Parisa and Pasha, were also with us for the puja.

After we did our puja, we all said "Happy New Year" and gave each other hugs! That's because Diwali is also the start of a new year for many people in the world. We get to say Happy New Year two times in the year! Because we celebrate a New Year, we also get new things like toys and clothes. I got a new blue race car and Kishyn got a green one. We all also got small building brick sets, and some new clothes. I wanted to play with my car, but Mama said we had to eat first.

HAPPY DIWALI

We all sat down to have a Diwali meal. Parisa, Kishyn, Pasha, and I sat at a little table next to the adults, just like at Thanksgiving. We also got to watch a Diwali video during our meal. We had so much yummy food – rice, paneer cheese tikka, dal, and roti – my super favorites. Dadi also made some Gulab Jamuns (sweet syrup treats) and I ate two. After a while, we all went to play and the adults kept eating. Parisa and I were building our brick sets and the little kids were playing with cars.

When dinner was done, we did sparklers with everyone outside. We all had so much fun and Kishyn and I even got to stay up a little late.

After a long day, Kishyn and I got ready for bed. "Read us a Diwali Book!" we cried. My Papa laughed and then said, "Why not!"

We read our favorite Diwali book and then laid our heads down to sleep.

After everyone left, we made sure we had a diya in every room to bless our home.

The next morning, I was still thinking of all the fun I had this Diwali, I love celebrating with my family, my friends, and now you as well.

Glad you could celebrate
Diwali with us!

See you next year!

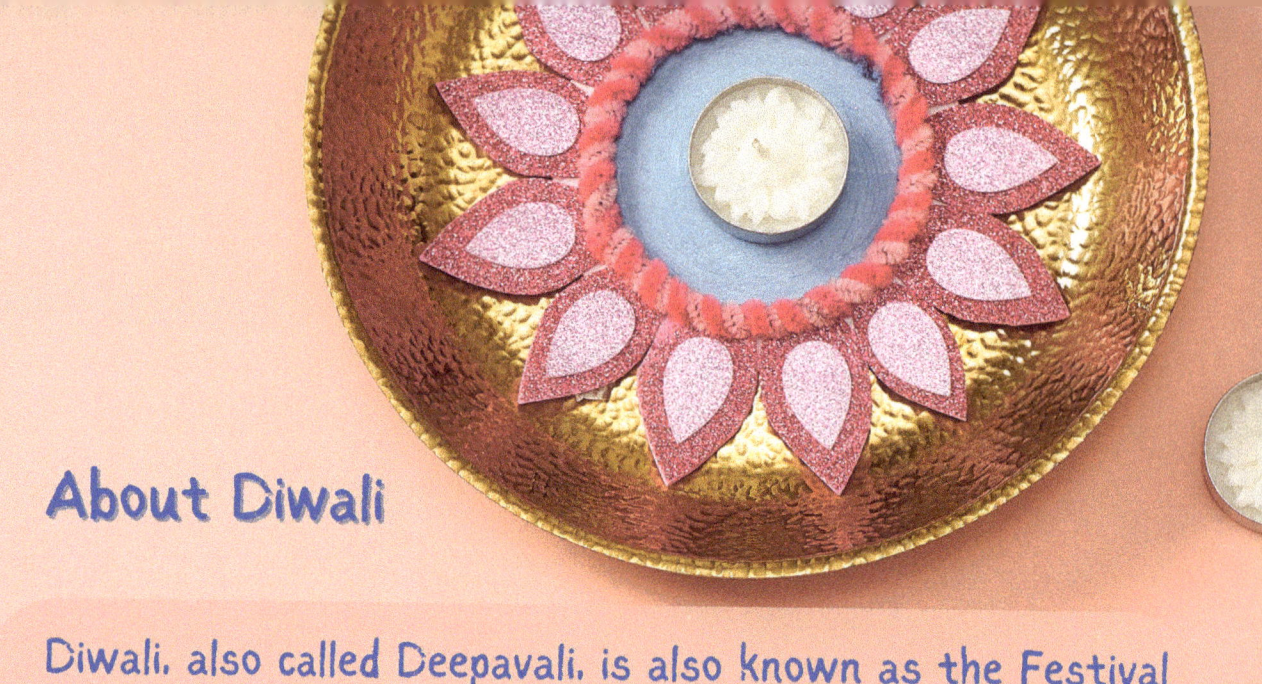

About Diwali

Diwali, also called Deepavali, is also known as the Festival of Lights. Diwali started as a celebration of the winning of good over evil, when Lord Rama, his brother Laxmana, and their friends defeated Ravana and ensured the safety of Princess Sita. When Rama, Sita, and Laxmana returned to their home there were grand celebrations and the town was lit up with diyas.

In modern times, Diwali is seen as a celebration of good over evil, and a time to pray for a prosperous year ahead. Families celebrate Diwali over five days, at home and with friends and family.

About Pujas

Ganesha God who is the Remover of Obstacles, and the first god prayed to in Hindu rituals to remove obstacles from the task ahead.

Laxmi Goddess of Prosperity, who is prayed to at Diwali. She sits on a lotus flower, which is a symbol of purity and spiritual growth.

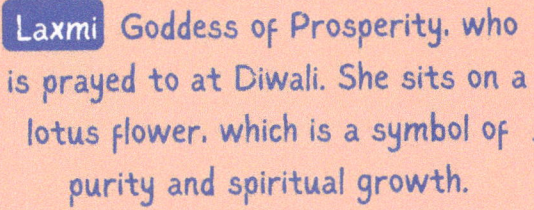

Abhishekam is a purifying ritual where you cleanse deities representing gods with different natural elements, including milk, honey, yogurt, and water. Abhishekam is performed in Hindu temples nearly every day, and is a ritual used to signify cleansing oneself when performed in the home.

Diya a small lamp often made of clay and filled with oil. Diyas are lit at pujas or at Diwali and other festivals.

Puja is a religious ceremony when Hindus pray to god by gathering around an image of god, performing rituals such as Abhishekam to purify and cleanse, and then praying and singing to god. Pujas can be performed in the temple or at home. The rituals often involve offering food to god, and then partaking in the "prasad" or blessed food to bless yourself. There are similar rituals in Christianity and other religions. Puja plates, or thalis, are typically set up with all of the offerings.

Relevant Mythology and Characters

The **Ramayana** is an epic Hindu story, detailing the life of Lord Rama, an avatar of the God Vishnu, present on earth. Rama was the eldest son of a king, strong and brave. He was married to Sita, who was the daughter of Mother Earth (also an avatar present on earth). When Rama was young, his step-mother became jealous of his good deeds, and convinced his father (the King) to exile Rama. Though Rama was upset, he went into the forest to live with his brother Laxmana and Sita by his side.

Rama, Sita, and Laxmana live in the forest, and coexist there. One day, Ravana kidnaped Sita and took her to his home in Lanka. Rama and Laxmana have to rescue Sita, and get the help of Hanuman to do so. Hanuman is the Monkey King, and, with his army, helped Rama defeat Ravana.

Soon after, Rama, Sita, and Laxmana returned to their home and the town celebrated. This day is Diwali, a day for celebrating good over evil, and light over dark, and the return of a beloved son.

Rama is the elder brother of his family, loved by all and next to be king, when he is suddenly exiled and sent to the forest to live because of family conflict. He is also an avatar of the God Vishnu.

Laxmana is Ram's devoted younger brother, who accompanies him to the forest as an act of service.

Ravana is a king among evil spirits. Ravana is smart and cunning, and kidnaps Sita one day to anger Ram. He takes her to his home, the then island of Lanka. Ravana was angered by and jealous of Rama, who many admired and desired, and therefore he kidnapped Sita.

Hanuman is the Monkey King, and devoted to Rama. With the help of Hanuman and his army, Rama was able to rescue Sita.

Sita is Rama's wife. She is captured in the forest one day by Ravana when he tricked her by appearing as a hurt deer.

Food Items

Ghee clarified butter

Laddoo a small round Indian sweet treat, made of nuts or flour and sugar, bound with ghee

Paneer homemade Indian cheese, often made into squares and cooked

Dal a soup made of lentils and spices, often eaten with rice or roti

Gulab Jamuns small fried donuts which are dipped in a warm sugar syrup

Roti a homemade wheat flatbread often eaten in North India, usually prepared on a flame

Sabji a vegetable dish often seen in a North Indian meal, made of spices and vegetables

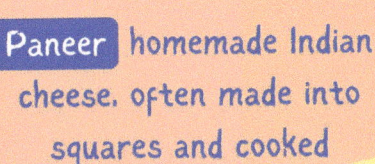

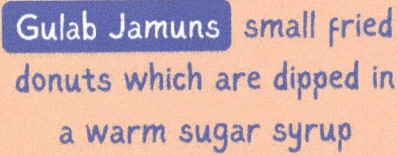

Jaiyen's Nani's Besan Laddoo Recipe

- Roast 2 cups of besan (chickpea flour) in a dry pan until fragrant
- Add 1 cup of powdered sugar, 1 tsp cardamom powder, and a pinch of salt to the pan
- Pour 1/2 cup ghee into the pan
- Combine and stir very well, until a nice paste is formed.
- Remove, cool, and roll into small balls. Top with chopped nuts, silver foil, or sprinkles.
- Serve with love.

Let the light within you shine as bright as the Diwali diyas.

About the Author

Parul L. Bhandari is a woman, born in the U.S. to first generation immigrants from India. Growing up, culture and rituals, especially around Diwali, were anticipated and celebrated with the community.

When Parul started visiting her children's classrooms as an adult, it was to share this culture further. However, at reading time, she could not always relate to the stories and characters. So, she set out to write a realistic story, based on Diwali activities she does with her children.

Parul is also a Customer Experience consultant, South Asian professional community leader, and a columnist for Inc.com. Her love of writing started at a young age, and has touched many forms such as poetry, fiction, and business writing.

Parul lives in Chicago with her husband and is "Mama" to her own Jaiyen and Kishyn.

www.ingramcontent.com/pod-product-compliance
Lightning Source LLC
Chambersburg PA
CBHW041543120626
46551CB00019B/2819